SAINT X

SAINT X

poems

Kirk Nesset

STEPHEN F. AUSTIN STATE UNIVERSITY PRESS
NACOGDOCHES ★ TEXAS

Stephen F. Austin State University Press
P.O. Box 13007, SFA Station
Nacogdoches, TX   75962-3007
sfasu.edu/sfapress
sfapress@sfasu.edu

Cover art: *Refuge* by Rob Evans
Author Photo: Nazli Inal
Book Design: Brittany O'Sullivan
Editor: Laura Davis
Manufactured in the United States of America

LIBRARY OF CONGRESS IN PUBLICATION DATA
Nesset, Kirk
Saint X / Kirk Nesset
p. cm.
ISBN: 978-1-936205-76-9

1. Poetry. 2. American Poetry 3. Kirk Nesset

The paper used in this book meets the requirements of ANSI/NISO
Z39.48-1992 (R1997) (Permanence of Paper).

ACKNOWLEDGMENTS

The following poems appeared, occasionally in slightly different form, in the following publications:

Antioch Review: "Some of the Most Striking Women I Have Known Have Been Men."
Boston Review: "I Will, I Will Not."
Chelsea: "Style," "Willing to Be."
Cimarron Review: "The House With No Glass and No Curtains."
Green Mountains Review: "Delirium."
Iowa Review: "Not Walter Pater."
Laurel Review: "Ultimate Sign."
Mid-American Review: "Contingency."
New England Review: "Catastrophe Road," "Stare."
New Orleans Review: "The Stinging and Saving."
Phoebe: "Madame Salvation," "The No-Theory Theory."
Ploughshares: "Time On the Down of Plenty," "Your Own Master," "Platinum Plus."
The Plum Review: "Integrity."
Plume Poetry Anthology 2012: "Dear Cat Drags In."
Poet Lore: "Erasing the Shadow" (published as "Thorn"), "France In Tahiti."
Prairie Schooner: "Saint X."
Quarterly West: "Island" (published as "I Hate to Hurt You").
Raritan: "Seven Essentials of Millennial People," "Sensitive Cargo," "Apology."
Spoon River Poetry Review: "Oh, Strikemaster!"
Writer's Forum: "The Collapse of the Heart is a Myth."

DEDICATIONS

"Some of the Most Striking Women I Have Known
Have Been Men" is for Barry Spacks.
"Seven Essentials of Millennial People"
and "Apology" are for Jesse.
"Poem" is for Maddie.
"Integrity" is for Emily Hogan.
"Locket" is for the inestimable Miss Normal.

CONTENTS

I WILL, I WILL NOT

*T*HE COLLAPSE OF THE HEART IS A MYTH

ERASING THE SHADOW

We are not saints, but we have kept our appointment.
How many people can boast as much?
— Samuel Beckett

From my fourth-floor room overlooking infinity, in the
viable intimacy of the falling evening, at the window
before the emerging stars, my dreams—in rhythmic accord
with the visible distance—are of journeys to unknown,
imagined, or simply impossible countries.
— Fernando Pessoa

Saints have no moderation, nor do poets, just exuberance.
— Anne Sexton

I WILL, I WILL NOT

In less pretty lives I plundered and razed,
son of the tankard and scabbard, boots grinding
dry straw, my brow in blue starlight, a pout-
faced child who pounds I will, I will not.
I was obese Lady Nelson, I sang the Admiral's
victories, quelling a riot in Naples
by the sheer force of voice; I was
Saint X, broken-ribbed, hung by the thumbs
for the sake of the bald and lame and corrupt.
I am Abdul and his nasty great aunt, Sir John
and his beard, I am the pond, the white trout
you let go — and strange Dr. Suess, no doctor
at all, living high on his hump in La Jolla
alone. In my unoccupied pocket are songs —
songs for those with less clutter —
for the still-blessed-by-ecstasy-and-nano-
technology, you who cruise the vacant rooms
of slow grace, waking, courting fresh dust.
This one's new but the same, one more roar
from the empty stadium, one more jovial prayer,
another flying charge at the unstillable heart,
so willful, whose silence we render
with clamor, more air.

TIME ON THE DOWN OF PLENTY

On Slaughter Beach I lay me down
on the sand between surf and calliope, there
where oceania meets glitz: plastic

mosques and minarets and transvestals, sub-
verts, countersexuals — Spanky Sparklenuts,
Afterbirth Boy and Crab Apple, Candace

the Grimace and She-Who-Eats-Only-Fish.
Nighttime it was, brine-sour, my head sunk
in shadow. Above, boardwalkers walked — catcalls

and titters. Such was my time on the down
of plenty; such is my way when inwardness
knells. How had I let myself poison

my passion? How had I failed to feel,
knees in the dust? What's done's done, said
my head — just do what you do. Mingle
with toothless epicures; enough moral
engorgement. The camel and gnat strain on
as they must. The sea, neon-tinged, hisses.

And the misshapen champion — feckless, un-
daunted, plucked — cavorts in his fiberglass grotto,
flexing his liver, his terrible guts.

CATASTROPHE ROAD

Have you spent eight strange years alone?
Are people concerned for your safety?

Do they now fail to call? Are you concerned
for your safety? Do you waver on Catastrophe

Road, emphasis and winking italics your own?
Are you addicted to sex? Do your soles burn

holes in cement? Has death moved into your
parlor, with his litter of ash, his meticulous wings?

Will you stay steadfastly bent, self-bludgeoned?
Will you still shamble through cinders and glass?

Must this be the finale? Will you not set your clock
while the wind rages? While the damage love did

resolutely undoes you? While, in the cornerless
morning, the unrelenting engines explode?

YOUR OWN MASTER

> The writer of our day has become
> especially repulsive recently by walking in
> public without his pants hind-end first and
> mournfully displaying to the world the
> place that hurts, and this place hurts him
> because he does not know where he can sit
> down peacefully.
>
> —*Maxim Gorky*

Down the hill past the bakery you air your affairs,
kicking beer cans and branches, clad in pink satin tank
top, pink socks. You skirt the amethyst edge;
you are assailed by dactyls; there is
irony yet to be milked. Thunderheads tweak the red
beard of summer, the bucolic trysts. In windows
in empty cafes napkins rest folded in castles
beside crystal glasses. A new load of pamphlets
hums in the satchel you clutch. You're Your Own
Master, one pamphlet states. Remember Flora
and Fauna, murmurs another. Above, at a casement,
someone hurls a tomato. A dead hit. Hot juice and
seed, hairy left cheek to hamstring. You maintain
the posture, head craning forward—the mad glitter
persists. Twelve hundred miles east, pilgrims stare
at the statue that stares at America. Swampy gardens,
darkling, darken, they go darker yet. Crows falter in.
The stricken sun fails to appear. Heaven minds
its own business. And still there is no place to sit.

SOME OF THE MOST STRIKING WOMEN I HAVE KNOWN HAVE BEEN MEN

At Brass Rail Cocktails at Fulton and 8th—
across from the block-long fake-granite bank—
they stare out through smoke, one muscular
leg crossed on the other, black hair tumbling
behind; the eyes haunt and enchant. At
the professional conference they quarrel,
so smart it hurts, decrying the jellyfish theory,
the orphic pronouncements, evangelical protestant-
ism, toadstools, the cannon and canon, skunks,
canine and feline, and later, Chester the six-foot mechanical
chicken, swiped by kids from a roof;
they hold difference aloft like a banner, they pause
to salute it. A dozen or so lifetimes ago, who was so watchful as
this? The hills humped their backs
in the rain, sprouting venomous flowers—the ocean snoring
and raving, at war with the glacier, the lean ghosts adrift,
capsized, capsized and raised, crashing their way
up the beach. Daughters and sons of oblivion, wielding
your scepters in Burbank and Kirkland, will you
still hunger, prey to the gnat and mosquito, will you
pawn your very lute for ten shillings? Will you still
say, dying of thirst in salt water, here's where you
finish, and here I begin?

THE BOAR AND SALT WATER

When one brittle sunflower peers from the dust,
when the dead sidle up to adjust us and the witnessing
stops, when questions turn to rows of tall needles,
the grim alarm fading in the unfeeling flood,
only then will I yield, unseamed from navel
to chops, my head stuck fast on a post,
unwept save by the tarpon and thrush; only
then, scalded and headless and dead will I pause,
will I fear the boar and salt water:
then, but not now while I rage,
while I thunder the plain with no destination,
trading each grotto of snow for the next, lips stained
catastrophically red, one freezing foot in Alberta
and one in Montana, there at the edge, where
the fine oiled gods boil still at dawn, bent
from not bending, uninterruptedly fighting—
fighting for, fighting against—fighting for smoke
and for skulls and for yams and for cattle, fighting
to keep these listless dead in their caves.

SEVEN ESSENTIALS OF MILLENNIAL PEOPLE

Defying the geese in Rochester, who harass you
for not bringing bread.

Avoiding Bloody Mary. Both before and after
her Caribbean cruise.

Hating and loving nativity scenes, each cheap piece
a beacon, each lit from within.

Killing your television.

Discovering Daido-shi backstage sneaking a smoke—
silently applauding his flaw, his mortal addiction.

Claiming My Will Be Done. Despite the truant
sun. Despite chronic fatigue syndrome.

Dipping your fingers in the river in winter;
in summer, in topsoil and mulch.

SENSITIVE CARGO

Mayflies breast the breeze-track of creek, lifting
and dipping. Hickory, willow, maple, catalpa—the mist
makes it Gainesborough, if deeper, more
muddy. Thrumcap, bullrush, blue heron
and spruce; a single recalcitrant cow.

Dusk. Silent you float. Your lure
hisses out, plips by the bank below a tree branch—
go ahead, reel. No one will chide, insisting This
has been done, Sir Isaac's met
Papa, come on: Enough sensitive cargo,

sensitive men, unhinged by sins
of the grape, waving that twenty-eighth of three thousand
        indulgences.
Reel, reel! No earthworm drowns at your bidding;
no iridescent minnow is stuck; the rare fish

you catch you release—an outraged smallmouth
or pike, diminutive, flailing.
Feel the chill heat in your grip, the cool
inner beat. The water and air the maples inhale
when, months later, ice settles in.

THAW

High on fear and cold air alone
you erected your fortress, ice-silver.
Spindles and gargoyles appeared, a ghost-
guard or two, while all the while the wheat

lay wincing beyond, wheat stubble, killed
again by the frost after the plagues of locusts
late summer. You savored the flavor of night-
mare, it seemed. Your titanium ramparts

were not safe to touch; touching yourself
meant layers of gloves. But here now you are
in the roar, cracking abruptly in the uproarious
thaw. Your gargoyles shudder, their

heads disengage, slip into their laps.
Why blame the rain, and the gray? In this new
add and removal you anticipate nothing. You
Return to Sender the skulls that arrive

in the mail. And circle back in your way,
recalling that mushroomy tree, the idle stag beetles
and ghosts of electricity, while the wheat breathes
beneath, dreaming the living promise of spring.

SKULL

Squat with your meat, if you must,
either for love or money, weigh
and consume; have at your baskets

of grapes and stumps; why trouble
your head about beggars in beds
taking pleasures as kings?

Who would preponderate thus?
Your kinsmen are apes but you
are immune: and come limping

up after, tattered receipt in
one hand, skull in the other,
balanced on forefinger and

thumb. Those who died didn't
die just to hurt you, prompting
this deluge of drink, air failing

to enter your lungs. What else
will serve? Will you still rise
with your flame-colored wings?

OH, STRIKEMASTER!

Asleep again in the bed of flowers I open
and bend, head cupped in the glow—rain mutters,
grubs till the brown earth. You appear
and say Up, I say Up where, you say Wherever
but move, and we move, unfolding the names
of the hues of the five wisdoms we know,
which are not marigold, iris, hydrangea, hibiscus
and rose, by the way, though these
are worth something and glow on their own.
Strikemaster who? I may ask—this man
we've been meaning to see, past the hill of teeth
and wide evergreen canyons. You'll answer the same:
no answer, no reason, we're moving too slow.
Oh, Strikemaster! come the volleying cries, and the news
of Strikemaster grows, while all around in the valley
there's thunder and torpor, and the rain moans
Don't follow, don't let it go.

*THE COLLAPSE OF THE
HEART IS A MYTH*

Landmasses form, sun warms the wet earth,

volcanoes issue pure fury, microbes appear
and I see it begin, trilobite, sea sponge, lungfish
and grouper, puffin and lemur and western fence lizard;
that sly big-headed ape, tool-user, losing fur in dry weather,
up on two legs to outrun the heat.

Mine is the voice of form and no matter—I fell extinct
before the Cretaceous. I see the experts agree, sipping
Gentleman Jack, unpacking fundamental quantum
mechanical problems, noses pressed to superconductors,
up to the elbows in psychic debris; I see hologram Lucy—
she stoops, still a little unwilling—coursing green plains
with her mate. What's dead comes apart, experts agree.
The tune disembodied is mute, no echo of fiber or bone
or post-fire synapse, no age of new chill portending, nor
arc or quiver in stillness: the collapse of the heart
is a myth.

I dwell underwater, hover and lurk
among armored sturgeonfish, evening spawners,
the popping pistol shrimp, the crunching parrotfish feeding,
and see the world disagree—and linger,
and spin old songs in the murk

BOZ DRINKS A BUMPER WITH JOHNSON TO SIR DAVID DALRYMPLE

Winter—gray inner weather—
prompts the sallying out. Ahead

stands the Heartbeat Convention; beyond,
Ashley's, veal and pudding and the threepenny bowl.

The snow does not lie on the ground
reddened with blood. At Turk's Head

the genius quaffs coffee, boots wiped,
palsied, thin glare of tear on his cheek.

Is disobedience still your first duty?
he queries. Sir, are the meditations hampered

by rodomontades? Still sorry
for the cocks at the cockfight, hoarding

your money? Why
this bandage in place of a smile?

CAFÉ PERPENDICULAR

After the rain routed us,
after crouching in stoops
with bums and trisexuals—
high on air and cascades,
mangling English and
French—we found the café
and pots of wine and
the time to kiss came
and we did and you hid
with your lips and wet
maps; and the wine tipped
in its white plastic cup,
and the man on the bike
we saw climbing the cloud-
shrouded mountain sails
head over wheels, unbrok-
en, unbruised; and whatever
you dabbed on my cheeks
in broad lines remains;
and in the rain's pulse
something still sings.

PROOF

Can we afford, like Celine, to piss
from a height? Indeed these are heart
and skull days. The trees grow shaggy
with snow. Will feeling too much
or too little calcify tissue? Shelley's
heart, no longer sea-soggy, wouldn't
ignite, was plucked from the ash pit
and shuffled—three decades, they say—
from Trelawny to Hunt or whoever
to Mary. Let the rats and tormentors
take note. The transparent ice-carrot,
tip dripping, lovely, snaps off rain gutters,
kills. The frozen rose is proof, exuding
its ruthless integrity. The point of each
point is that the points are all moot.
The rock solid heart, storm-tossed,
at one end, and meltdown beyond,
waves of inexhaustible light.

STYLE

She stood and delivered, those nights on
the jetty—she rattled in Sino-Korean, all
headpiece and crutch, free finger testing
the jet stream. The sand held its breath,
the bream and surf perch were stunned.
Death is but a question of style, she averred—
something in her averred—and questions
of style are best left unanswered,
unquestioned.

No sermons, she groaned, but notice
the jellyfish armies, the beach flea, the gribble
and limpet, this cryptic rabble of pebbles.
She capered, intoning, she whistled—we know
no Korean—directing us back to our silks
and damp darkness, our potato pots,
our fear of transcendence.

She adheres to her jetty, unfettered; we leave her
alone. She howls out her syllables. *Style, style!*
she shrieks. We answer, far off, but the words
fail to settle. We're dying, we think.

MADAME SALVATION

She invented the barbot,
bee-eater, and demoiselle crane;
she sat six years in Mecca, silent,
three in White Plains.
No dispensation, she murmurs—
a soul is marked Finished, Do Not
Recycle, in time.
She vibrates on Market
amidst the machines, hot
metal, rubber, aquamarine.
The wind lilts, the sky fades
to plum. God swings
from eaves in tall buildings,
unbent by heartache, by
irresistible terrestrial love.

THE NO-THEORY THEORY

Translucent, small as rice grains, unmoving,
they dot walkways and lawns, porch railings,
decks, hoods of vehicles, millions riding in
on the rain—and while science jabs the glass

slide with tweezers, nobody knows what they
are. There's the airborne chemical spill theory,
Chinese conspiracy theory, and blown-to-bits-
jellyfish theory, spores sucked from the Sound

in offshore cluster bomb tests to cloud-quiver
down on the town. We moan about omens,
God's gelatinous tears. And endure hair
loss, heartworm, hives, diarrhea, nostalgia,

burning bladder, immaculate births.
We have unpleasant dreams involving
rodents and heavy equipment. We didn't
ask to be sick. We are not zealots or evil

but mind our business, our rhododend-
rons and coffins, nudging the universe
like everyone else, squashing yawns back
with our teeth. We want facts. This is

the twenty-first century, this is not Asia,
we have boats here and grass to the water,
from Sharktooth and Heather to Humming-
bird Lane. We need details, not lies about

cells with no nucleii. Maria wails for a tail-
pipe, a bumper, an eyehole. Demented child-
ren embrace. Rain taps our shoulders, our
hats. Theory by theory the theories deflate.

CONTINGENCY

Stranger, we meet again on a street
in your city, my mangled bumper raised
in a sneer. You plead, but what can

we say? We married young. We
honored the hornbill and greenback and god
of the flask, founded the United Church

of Intense, and battled, reviling
meadow and woods. We unmasked
the masked man, that wriggler and wag,

exposed his sacred baboon. You blew
a tire, wept briefly; I burned up an engine.
We witnessed the bent dried bodies,

voluptuous crucifixions, while the sun
shone red through the windows. And
here now you stand with your corduroy face
between the lamp post and one-legged pigeon,
bandaged, ignoring our straightforward
peace. Stand farther off. Move.

I'm done with blood ink and quicksand,
canker, contingency—take back
Samarkand and Kabul and Ho Chi Min
City, the sullen dead and mud-sullied
wounded, half-sunk, so many.

AFFAIR-PROOF YOUR MARRIAGE:
A MANUAL (INSTALLMENT SEVEN)

Beware the darker inner cosmologies. A single tumble
of touch signals the scramble of something momentous.

Don't wax the saddle at the expense of the horse.

Empty pedestals abound. So do venom-dipped shafts.
Aim your bow, if you must, at your foot.

Buy your hair shirt at Penny's, not Macy's. Buy it
large enough to accommodate two.

Remember—but do not pity—Liz Taylor.

Remain prince or princess aboard your wooden world.
Sail on. Love and mirth are not your business in Naples.

Suspect formulas, tonics, elixirs, tinctures, plasters, remed-
ies, therapies, quinines of lime and catharses, quarantines,
tourniquets, intoxicants, snake handlers, binders, analysts,
guides and knife-grinders and other glib if respectable coun-
sel. Go in fear of professionals. Manuals. Professional
manuals.

Exhale. Assess. Caress the beloved. Empty the pail of con-
fetti you guard by the bed.

Let wild violets whisper their secrets. Why
pry? Why bend to insist?

ISLAND

Once again: no. I'm more memory
than meat, all shadow, no body

attached in gray daylight, just
one last opulent whisper;

I drown in your kitchen,
pretending to swim.

We shared the language,
agreed. And saw

the mustard-bright star
near the moon, and curled,

bare forked things in the dark.
But no more.

I mumble my way back
to Ithaca now.

All night I rained
and the island is sinking,

sinking. Gone. Already
gone.

FRANCE IN TAHITI

Daily I recheck the wreckage. I lift
and inspect, probing spectacular failures,
scraping frescoes from walls to mix with water
for medicine.

Here where there's vision and sense, where
there's breadfruit and grapes and waves
of persimmons—here in the shimmer
I pause, forecasting rain

when it's raining. I keep the cup
partly empty to allow for more filling.
Van Gogh we know scared women off
with the knife-edge of fervor;

Gauguin survived with mistress and monkey,
daring all to do all, aching for Tahiti in France,
France in Tahiti. Lautrec stalked the demi-monde,
hobbling, clutching bent sticks; and

tidy dapper Mondrian, newly arrived
in New York, inhaling bebop and swing,
thought enough was enough and shot
every last self-portrait dead

with a gun. There's meaning it seems
in the way things undo us, in the way
the wheels click neatly, politely
together.

Dreaming, I take on the freeways again,
follow arrows around trunks of magnolias.
I'll die, if need be, of poisoned meat
at the feedings. What are cures

but assaults on the false and infected? What
but this bloodless snip and sweep, this slow
redirection, this detouring back
on routes that we know?

STARE

Because trees can be coy about how, where and when
they fruit, because things blur in the canopy, we perfect
that infinite look, directed outward, not in.

Because bandits lurk, because gunmen cling to black-
flanked taxis, we're all arboreal eyes,
silently surreptitiously breathing. Raiding, they addle

the ferns, they curse, they break pottery. The sun
sleeps in their camouflage caps. Highway and seaport
are lost. Tropical mold holds more in store for

itself than we do for the future. And what
bent concept might one erect for an cause?
We're diluted to near-invisibility, ensconced

on branches. Blind pineapples ripen. The moon
peeps, dawn ordains the morning. We
wait, watching. The fruit rots where it drops.

I AM NOT WALTER PATER

I am not Walter Pater, morbidly sniffing
the old spilled religion, always elsewhere
when the hammer drops, flaring gem-like

in lemon kid gloves and silk apple-green tie,
viewing the hill of teeth from a distance.
I'm not James or Jane Austen or Hopkins,

Empson, Dr. Fowles from Cal State L. A.
I swallow fear and dry oats, embrace
the pay-per-view juries, predictable edicts,

the lessons you learn but will not adopt,
if more or less cherish—another poor soul
face down in raw sewage, perversely unwhole,

perversely on foot while the saddled horse follows,
half bitten in half, still shadowed by hill,
heart stuck awake in its socket.

WILLING TO BE

> In the desert there is no sign that says,
> Thou shalt not eat stones.
> > —*Sufi proverb*

Do not regret the passing of the caravan and the camel.
The candle will weep its wick away anyway, pale hills

will go black, the moon will roll out on tiptoe. What,
more thoughts of slaughter? Noon prayers first Repose.

Then rampage—rocks and bricks and broken bank windows,
the burnt car, overturned, and burnt truck. Let

Information Minister Marwan Muasher
in his voice of raw egg white deny it,

the riot, let the price of wine and bread rise.
Draw water from cactus; make a soup of these stones.

How alive, truly, are you willing to be?
The bell tolls. Willows still harmonize

wind. Silence, starsick,
unfolds.

ERASING THE SHADOW

The universe is lumpier than experts assumed,
sliding sideways as well as expanding,
suns flaring and fading.

I float on in the haze, the lavender
air, aware of the lemon and rose,
the blackberry ripening,
tilting, orbiting nothing.

I raise my cup to the thorn, to the sage
and half-sorry, drinking in air, drinking in water,
buying innocence back, a bland statue,
Patience, humped and deflated;
I empty myself out for you.

And scratch my name in damp sand
as waves flee the daylight,
erasing the hyphen between us,
erasing the shadow.

ROOM

I will not let light slant
over my unmeasured
corners, abandoned by
butchers who spare

not one single lamb;
nor will the bookshelves
presume, will I call upon
Pound, Pepys, Margaret

Atwood or Homer, the
wide jars of words, wet
seed pods of pleasure—
not while time ticks

its perfume, whiter
than blue, and there's
air here, and room,
night prompting

these haphazard
glimpses of you.

APOLOGY

See me revolve, white quartz and gold. I tilt,
dear heart, in your orbit—I hiss past

in my armaggedon sedan. My floorboards,
indeed, are rusted; my blinker is stuck. But

proximity's luxury. Who wouldn't savor your
headshake and sneer, your bastion, unbreak-

able padlocks, the fact that you swallow
keys? Who wouldn't choose

your luster over the pressure of fear?
Welcome to my intergalactic R-rated

movie. See me promenade, good female
Friday. Take my boysenberry candle,

my orchid, my purple quill duster. Just
let me strut in your space, that's all

I ask, backfiring, belching, rich as ripe
amber, untouched by pain or apology.

Someone kiss accidently
a fungus. A brown lip
claim you did not.

HIATUS

An apology for not mention
I am on hiatus these months.
I peddle my friendly whatever
so worry me. Even we never
met is reasons I did not stop
myself up.

I went a phase (many went
going through), the phase
of Identity! Moment in
life (weeks!) trying to find
the identity! Peeling skin
and soul outside cliché
inside surrounding.

I wish you translate me
a blog have a fig break-
fast is served enjoy a big
weekend. Sell the cells!
Mummies waiting for
pyramid!

Have you been a child?
The sun so hot is raw,
the moon hating heating
the wife living heartburn
the children painting with sauce.

THING

It leapt from malt liquor
in Emblem, Wyoming, learned
to stand in lake mud, half-sunk,
amidst skulls of gars; it grew up
lapping the tarpaper roof
with its tongue.

Lately it grunts, grunts
as it squats in the headlands,
fog-drenched, among the bulwarks
and bottle necks and bicycle kick-
stands, investing lost seconds
with salt, sunk to the chest
and white knuckles.

It demands its bread
as it were without butter—
outraged, aggrieved, aggrieved
and outraged by you, rough and blunt
and uncouth, a preposterous unpacifiable
thing, a slobbering mountain, squatting
or not, this thing of the dark
you've begun to reclaim.

Even now you hear it
call out, you hear it calling
purposively, pleading. It's weeping
in its grimacing way, plucking its ten thousand
spikes with its teeth, long lavender spurs
that not only burn but kill
when they sting.

THE STINGING AND SAVING

The old gourmands are dead. The new scavenge loaves
and boot heels from dumpsters, ready to scatter, pausing

to shake scales from their wrists. The butterscotch days,
not sadly, are over; so is cornflower blue. Snowflakes

whisper the code names, the mockingbird mocks the car
alarm sound. The curtains in the house of the metaphysician

are torn, the door boarded up, but the man's ghost is still bent
by the curb with its one shoe and pencil, head stuck in a trunk.

For the man with the beaker, high on his mesa, loss has body
and weight. He's reading time backwards, cornering random

free floating quarks; he's raising the scorpion that drowns
in the pail. And angels all around in the world loiter

and stare, observing the discarded cork, the bread crust,
the mask and the spear, the columns and caves at Lascaux.

THE HOUSE WITH NO GLASS AND NO CURTAINS

Return to the house with no glass
and no curtains, no screens

at the windows, white walls
stark against that backwater

maze—the only way in
is by boat.

You've known it forever
but can't possibly know.

See the people you failed,
they range in a circle,

see how they hold out
their cups.

Dry palm branches rattle;
moon streams through holes

in the roof. Drop a bean
in each cup, feel

yourself lift, pure flight
and intention—then reenter

the circle, hailing fire
and misfire in this headlong

careening, this painful
human career.

SAINT X

We were born under punches, too thin,
pugnacious in wartime, shaken awake
by rattles and flares; we traced dot-to-dot
faces in patterns of stars. Then came

Hitchcock and Perkins, a generation
of women forsaking hot baths, then the flag
on the coffin and thirty million who wept; then
came Saint X, holy to all and to no one:
straitjacket, pickpocket, backbiter, bawd.

Both ends against the middle, you said—
why play? Nakedly sane, we relearned
the daisy, bare toes and loam and the beard,
electric puce and flamingo, crying
I defy you to try to sanitize me.

Movies on fifty-cent night, rain drumming
the quonset-hut roof, no eggs in our basket,
no egg yoke at our feet. We thumbed it
to Sunrise, to Meadville and Wheeler, without

and within the machine; we slept among
tombstones in churchyards in Spain. I'll do
and I'll do and I'll do, I decreed, passing dill
and wild eglantine, loving pain for the way
it clarified me, and you for making failure
look perfect, loving the air for being

more blue than yellow, the earth
for refusing to swallow.
We did and we did, blindly alive
in our dreaming, at war with the middle,
riding the roar like Trauffaut on a truck
on the beach with his camera, tires
deflated to absorb the vibration.

DEAR CAT DRAGS IN

How was our nondescript week?
Is hollow still hollow? Has
the corn ripened, do stars

graze the lake? Dear ghoul,
dear seizure, venom, dear
what not to do when flattening

Rome, stand farther off—
avaunt, avoid, recede—
feast elsewhere, anywhere

but where what was
is concerned. Take back
your oaks and dusk

and barbed wire and bleach,
your litter of ash and à chacun
ses gouts: take back this

vertiginous world.

POEM

The poem was doomed
but determined to live,
adoring your dress
with its zigzagging skulls
and too full of thunder,

which melodramatically
cracked as we parked,
and I, the bow-hunting
rock god, battled the flood
to buy hard lemonade.

It seemed to want
to convey our illustrious
end, which hasn't yet
happened; it gestured,
it gibbered and mowed,

it drove enigmatically slow
on the freeway; it said I
am all alone in this room
and I am less damaged
than some.

What it couldn't begin
to convey, wedged
against the faux-Romanesque
church, stopping to pee
in its picturesque alley,

bleeding drafts of itself
in fits on the long drive
back—what it couldn't
say simply cannot be
said: itself enough

to insist on this
late summer storm,
your pale perfect hands
in the storm, our
ongoing poem.

DELIRIUM

If I could live in the furrow
I would. Tomorrow'd sink
like the past and what sank
would stay buried, would
fade into peach-tinted light.

At root it's failure to steer,
the plow veering off blindly
to haphazardly slice.

If I could live inside—unerring—
I would: beyond the bugbears
and dead inward glimpse,
twelve thousand miles
from Horseheads, NY,
the horned stink ant and razors.

Call it broken-wing grace,
call it precarious thistle—I recoil,
totter. The untilled dark
is too dark to enfold. New hills
rise a half step behind.
Nothing to do now but swerve,
nowhere to go but awry.

INTEGRITY

Among chimneys and telephone wires
you spy out imposter camps—
nothing survives. I reclaim

my virginity, swollen on breadfruit
and groats, eggplant, the irreproachable
peach; you rebuild columns at Trajan.

I bathe in prosperity, unburied, unwept;
you make elms and raingutters hum.
We sip cheap beer on the bench

(God emits not a murmur), loving
the raven, the jay's frantic beak, we
hitchhike, backslide, unpack a theory,

cry and then cease, hopelessly hope-
ful, perfecting this ruthless integrity.
Don't stand close to hot oil, goes

the warning. Don't use that bent knife
to preach. The water, the wind, you insist—
hear the blackberry sigh as it tips.

You lift the paintbrush, the porthole,
the scepter. I kiss the ghost
in my sleep.

MR. TRANSCENDENT

And yet here he sits, twelve hundred feet up
with his hat, lolling in rabbitgrass and Abraham
fennel, beyond the pond and cane garden, lips
effervescent with pollen.

What else would you have the man do? Sip
iced lemon tea in air-cooled hotels? Eat peach pie
for lunch a la mode? Should he glide the long length
of strand, admire its bouquets of banners and pink

molar cliff, its odd spray of phenomena, floating
bistro to bistro on tiptoe, pondering menus?
No, let him let go, high on his hill—let the self
slide off like skin, as it does when it can, let him

pause where he is, unmindful of mindsets yet
to begin, sprawling in clover and imperturbable
fennel. Let him wear the bent hat, let him eat
dry oats and sky while down the hill and beyond

roses stand dead on their stems, and Jupiter dims,
and ships haunt the bay—while down the hill
and beyond the blind die for love, and the rest
stay steadfastly unhappy.

LOCKET

If I were the wind, I'd braid and unbraid
your hair, rearranging what hasn't settled,

freeing myself from myself, loving your
eyes and lips and swollen toe, the mark

on your arm shaped like New Zealand.
If I were gold, I'd be the locket you lost

in a wide field of mud; I would meet sun-
rise and shake its hand gently, apprehend-

ing your dreaming, unsleeping, repeating
your name until the unraveling ends,

until names and naming are done.

ULTIMATE SIGN

In summer when white grubs drill the earth
I see the end of the world—not visions,
not hills of skulls agitated by fog, not cactus
or rock; not one burning shrine honoring pain
or one man alive in his cave at high tide.

Previews, not visions—no long-running
display, no show of duration. Just smoke
and dry grass, fragments of canyons
of bone, ripe silence, thunder. In Dracut
and Pittsburgh brick factories fall; men
wipe dust from the leaves of plastic plants
in cafes. In Emblem, Wyoming, new
stern horizons go inky with rain.

Nobody stirs. Ultimate signs, shamans
will say, reeling, repairing the meaning,
replanting gods in the strawberry patch,
revealing Saint X in the strawberry light.

Nazli Inal

AUTHOR BIOGRAPHY

Kirk Nesset is author of two books of fiction, *Mr. Agreeable* and *Paradise Road*, as well as *Alphabet of the World: Selected Works by Eugenio Montejo* (translations) and T*he Stories of Raymond Carver* (nonfiction). A recipient of the Drue Heinz Literature Prize, a Pushcart Prize, and grants from the Pennsylvania Council on the Arts, Nesset has published widely; his poems, stories and translations have appeared in *The Paris Review, Kenyon Review, Southern Review, Gettysburg Review, Iowa Review, Boston Review, American Poetry Review, Ploughshares, Crazyhorse, Agni, Prairie Schooner, The Sun, Witness* and elsewhere—including three of W. W. Norton's short-short story anthologies: *Flash Fiction Forward, New Sudden Fiction* and *Sudden Fiction Latino.* He teaches at Allegheny College, and serves as writer-in-residence at Black Forest Writing Seminars (Freiburg, Germany).

CPSIA information can be obtained at www.ICGtesting.com
Printed in the USA
LVOW040818101012

302204LV00003B/1/P